The Top Effective Communication Skills You Should Know About

LAURA MORALES

Copyright © 2024, LAURA MORALES,
All right Reserved

Table of content

Introduction
Chapter 1
Chapter 2
Chapter 3
Chapter 4
Chapter 5
Chapter 6
Chapter 7
Chapter 8
Conclusion

Introduction

One of the most important life lessons is communication, which someone who masters might find life to be really easy. In business, efficient communication facilitates smooth operations and prevents a host of potential issues down the road.

An average firm lost $62.4 million annually in production due to poor communication, according to a research that included 400 organizations from the USA and the UK.

However, you may be asking what "effective communication" really means. Determining the information's genuine meaning is essential to effective communication. It entails figuring out what the user is attempting to convey to you and how. It also entails our speaking or responding to a user in a way that makes sense to them.

But a lot of people lack the abilities necessary for clear communication. We'll be looking at the top abilities necessary for successful communication.

Chapter 1

The Top Skills for Effective Communication are listed as below:

Pay close attention when others are speaking

One of the most important components of good communication is listening. Active or involved listeners gain a deeper understanding of the subject matter. It indicates that even when a speaker is not very successful, engaged listeners still grasp what the user is attempting to express.

People occasionally pay little attention to what other people have to say, especially in the job. They either don't listen intently or disregard it. All of this results in the loss of important information and lessens the essence required for efficient communication.

Additionally, recognizing the speaker's present attitude and goals is much easier when you are an engaged listener. Thus, establish a stronger link for more fruitful conversation. To foster trust among your team members, it's essential to listen intently.

How can one listen intently?
Maintain appropriate eye contact with the speaker and pay attention to their words and expression in order to be an attentive listener. There are plenty of questions you may ask if you're still unclear. However, it is not advisable to interrupt for your own gain, so be sure to do this after the discussion has concluded. To engage in active listening, pay attention and maintain good posture.

Oral exchanges

The skill of efficiently communicating your thoughts, feelings, and ideas using language and words is known as **verbal communication.** It's an essential ability that's important in many facets of life. You'll be able to communicate better in both personal and professional settings. You can also do really well in public speaking situations.

Effective verbal communication is built on the foundation of careful and clear speaking. The manner you speak has a big influence on how people hear and comprehend what you're trying to say.

To do this, you have to:
~ Be mindful of the way you pronounce each word.

~ To enhance your expressiveness, work on your pronunciation using activities.

~ Set a speaking tempo that is comfortable for you. Speaking too slowly might engender indifference, while speaking too rapidly can make you hard to follow.

~ Plan your pauses carefully. Key points may be emphasized by using pauses. It will also benefit you to give your audience time to process the material or take a little break to collect your thoughts.

~ Add more terms to your vocabulary to increase its variety. You'll be able to communicate concepts more clearly and fluidly with practice.

~ Learning to adjust your tone and pitch is another crucial factor to take into account here. Your voice's tone and pitch are effective instruments for evoking feelings in your listeners and building connection.

In order to communicate verbally effectively, you must modify your tone and pitch to fit the subject and intent of the discussion or presentation.

Chapter 2

Be succinct

Being concise in communication means that you can express your ideas clearly and succinctly. It is usually preferable to arrange your ideas before writing or speaking. This is due to the fact that more productive and clearer thinking always result in better communication.

The goal of communication is to use clear, concise language wherever possible. Keeping your message simple to understand is more important than impressing with intricacy in this situation.

Consequently, it's critical to constantly steer clear of extraneous terms and details that might confuse the meaning of your message.

Above all, your speech should be valuable with every word you say.

Be specific and unambiguous

To be a good communicator, you need also understand how to convey your ideas clearly and concisely. You cannot be a good communicator if you are someone who offers a whole untrue backstory without providing any evidence to support your claims.

On the other hand, your audience will understand you more clearly if you are particular in your message. In order to be concrete with your message, you must also include specific specifics, such as facts and numbers, concerning the material you are presenting.

Additionally, you must convey your message clearly. To help others understand you more clearly and quickly, you want your message to be concise and well-defined. A message's clarity is essential since it guarantees that every team member will be able to comprehend you without difficulty. Use an energetic voice, a basic vocabulary, and clarity in your goals when speaking to ensure that your message is understood. Speaking the same language as your audience is also beneficial. These days, you may study Spanish, French, German, and other foreign languages more quickly thanks to technology.

Chapter 3

The secret is communicating nonverbally (body language)

For you to communicate effectively, your body language is essential. Although your words have weight, your tone, eye contact, facial emotions, and hand gestures hold greater significance. Making hand motions when speaking conveys strength and confidence. Therefore, it enables the other person to focus on you and genuinely hear what you have to say.

Speaking while utilizing non-verbal cues facilitates deeper interpersonal relationships and more efficient and effective message delivery. Develop your understanding of various hand gestures, tones, and attitudes to enhance your nonverbal communication.

To better understand the message, be mindful of other people's nonverbal cues as well.

Undoubtedly, it is among the Top Critical Skills for Effective Communication. This cannot be disregarded.

Self-assuredness

The capacity to respectfully and boldly convey your needs, wants, and feelings is known as assertiveness in communication. Try expressing your ideas and emotions with "I" phrases. Say, instead of "This approach is better," "I believe this approach is more effective."

You should also continue to communicate in a forceful yet courteous manner. Aggression is not the same as assertiveness. It's because it expresses your viewpoint in an unambiguous and straightforward manner.

You have to be able to politely express your thoughts when needed. It is imperative that you never back down from advocating for your values, even if doing so means resolving confrontations or disagreements.

Be at ease

Anxiety and tension can demotivate you and impede your ability to communicate. You may be an inefficient communicator as a result of one of these two factors.

Effective communication requires relaxation and a stress-free environment. You make poor word choices when you're under stress. It complicates matters for your audience to comprehend you.

Additionally, maintaining your composure and lack of tension throughout a conversation aids in your understanding of its nature. It also assists you in deciding between fight and flight mode. Here, "fight or flight" refers to responding or remaining silent, depending on the circumstances.

Furthermore, maintaining a calm attitude guarantees that you make choices that you won't regret down the road and steer clear of many issues. Therefore, maintaining composure is advised in order to speak successfully.

Chapter 4

Notify

You must explain the topic of your conversation to your audience if you want to be a successful communicator. Giving your listeners a basic overview of the conversation might be beneficial. It would also make it easier for them to understand the information.

In addition, you should let your audience know what important details or topics they should pay attention to and remember during the discussion.

By explaining the topic of the conversation to others, you set the stage for your audience to understand you and assist them in taking the appropriate action. Since not every member of your audience has the same level of knowledge as you, you should also take the time to fully clarify your arguments to them. Being able to articulate your ideas and thoughts clearly to a variety of audience groups makes you a more successful communicator.

Flexibility

Being adaptable in communication entails changing your approach depending on the circumstances and the individuals involved. Through a variety of techniques, you may also improve your capacity to adjust in conversation. You'll definitely need the following advice in this situation:

Always be mindful of other people's preferences and communication methods. Knowing your audience's particular requirements and expectations is the first step toward being adaptable.

\# Adjust your communication style as necessary. It implies that you have to adjust your message to the audience you are speaking to, whether they be members of a varied group, people with various personalities, or different organizational hierarchies.

\# You should also be willing to make changes and continue to be receptive to criticism.

All things considered, becoming more adaptive requires constant work, and honing your communication style is a useful quality in and of itself. Consequently, in order to convey your message as effectively as possible, it is always necessary to use feedback constructively and develop your flexibility abilities.

Chapter 5

Have a visual

Giving your audience a visual representation of the information you want them to see can help them retain it longer. Human psychology is ingrained with the idea that we digest information far more quickly than it is represented by visuals.

A research found that people are better than other animals in deciphering and retaining visual information.

The same study came to the conclusion that words are not retained in our memory for as long as visuals are. Therefore, in order to be a good communicator, you need to be able to help your audience understand what you're saying. To achieve this, it's recommended that you use appropriate information-delivery techniques, such as visual communication. Information may be represented visually using graphs, pictures, maps, and charts.

Be compassionate

Empathy is the same as understanding. Sometimes what you say or how you feel contradicts other people or team members. But you shouldn't be upset or annoyed in this kind of circumstance. Rather, honor their viewpoint and be in awe of their bravery. Consider it a healthy form of rivalry.

Use phrases like "I understand what you are trying to say, but..." or "Sorry, but I think..." to demonstrate exceptional comprehension and ensure that others view you as a competitive communicator. Making remarks such as these would encourage people and let them know you were listening to what they had to say.

Chapter 6

Narrative

Arguably, one of the most crucial communication abilities to captivate and influence people is the ability to tell stories. When mastering storytelling for more effective and captivating communication, there are a number of factors to take into account.

You should, for instance, create a story that has a distinct beginning, middle, and finish. Organize your narrative to grab the reader's attention and successfully deliver your point. Make use of clear language and visuals to help your audience visualize what you're talking about. To make your narrative unforgettable, it will assist you in appealing to their senses and emotions.

You also need to practice telling stories in a variety of settings. The ability to tell stories effectively is a flexible talent that can be developed over time, whether it be for marketing campaigns, personal narratives, or corporate presentations.

To become a better storyteller, you need continue practicing.

Wholeness

When communicating, being complete implies finishing your statements. Occasionally, you could see that someone begins a statement. However, after a little while, they get so perplexed that they stop addressing the first argument and begin discussing others. As a result, everything about it is extremely confusing and hinders clear communication.

You must fully and precisely clarify the first point before moving on to the next in order to communicate successfully. A link and logical inference must exist inside the phrases, and you must present your ideas in a sequential manner.

Moreover, it is especially important when responding to someone else, as being thorough simplifies and organizes a lot of conversational exchanges. Therefore, it is imperative that you hone this talent if you want to be an excellent communicator.

Chapter 7

Resolution of Conflicts

The skill of efficiently managing and resolving conflicts to foster understanding in a variety of contexts, including interpersonal relationships, the workplace, and community interactions, is known as conflict resolution. Acquiring the ability to resolve conflicts may be very beneficial in both personal and professional contexts.

Honest conversation may be fostered via open communication. A secure environment where all parties feel heard and respected is necessary for effective conflict resolution and facilitates the identification of underlying problems.

As a result, in order to develop dispute resolution as a communication ability, you must do the following:

When in disagreement, maintain your composure and rationality. When handling difficult situations, emotional intelligence is essential.

Make sure you hear all viewpoints on the matter. It is crucial to comprehend the viewpoints of all parties involved in order to identify common ground and settle any disagreement amicably and successfully.

In addition, it emphasizes finding solutions that benefit all parties rather than focusing on winning at the expense of oneself. In conflict resolution, win-win solutions promote wholesome bonds and productive team dynamics.

Provide and Get Input

Feedback-giving and -taking are fundamental to good communication and are considered key competencies. Giving feedback boosts one's confidence, while getting some in return enables you to identify and strengthen your areas of weakness.

Not every comment will be positive and compliment you on who you are as a person. Although they might be difficult to read at times, you must respond positively to them in order to improve as a communicator. Additionally, make an effort to comprehend the issues that are motivating the input that individuals are providing. If you are having trouble understanding the feedback, you may also ask the senders what they mean.

Chapter 8

Sensitivity to Culture

Being aware of and respectful of other people's cultural norms and values is the foundation of cultural sensitivity. You have to be considerate of the cultural values of others in all of your communications. You should take into account the following practical advice in order to adjust to cultural sensitivity:

It is advisable that you familiarize yourself with many cultures and practices. Take the time to become knowledgeable about the customs, histories, and beliefs of many communities.

Avoid presumptions and preconceptions about people based on their cultural background. Never forget that every person is different and that making generalizations might cause offence and misunderstandings.

Above all, it's best to keep an open mind and be eager to absorb knowledge from others with different viewpoints. Here, interacting with people from diverse cultural backgrounds and looking for opportunities to increase your awareness of other cultures can also be successful strategies.

Make use of your insensate approach

You need to know your teammates in order to communicate with them in the workplace or in your line of business.

Therefore, don't squander the valuable time you have during your lunch or coffee break by eating by yourself. Use that time wisely to learn more about your coworkers so you can get to know them better.

You would be able to interact with your team members more effectively the more knowledge you have about them.

Conclusion

In conclusion, the most important abilities for effective communication are listed above. Gaining these abilities will improve your ability to interact with people.

www.ingramcontent.com/pod-product-compliance
Lightning Source LLC
Chambersburg PA
CBHW070958220526
45471CB00007B/3091